"STOPS" OR, HOW TO PUNCTUATE

A Practical Handbook for Writers and Students

MJP
PUBLISHERS

"STOPS" OR, HOW TO PUNCTUATE

A Practical Handbook for Writers and Students

PAUL ALLARDYCE

London, T. Fisher Unwin Ltd.

Adelphi Terrace.

Chennai   New Delhi   Tirunelveli

ISBN 978-81-8094-325-6

MJP Publishers

No. 44, Nallathambi Street,

Printed and bound in India

Triplicane, Chennai 600 005

MJP 264

© Publishers, 2018

Publisher : **C. Janarthanan**

Project Editor : **C. Ambica**

"For a reader that pointeth ill, A good sentence oft may spill."

—*Chaucer—Romaunt of the Rose*

PUBLISHER'S NOTE

The legacy of a country is in its varied cultural heritage, historical literature, developments in the field of economy and science. The top nations in the world are competing in the field of science, economy and literature. This vast legacy has to be conserved and documented so that it can be bestowed to the future generation. The knowledge of this legacy is slowly getting perished in the present generation due to lack of documentation.

Keeping this in mind, the concern with retrospective acquiring of rare books has been accented recently by the burgeoning reprint industry. MJP Publishers is gratified to retrieve the rare collections with a view to bring back those books that were landmarks in their time.

In this effort, a series of rare books would be republished under the banner, "MJP Publishers". The books in the reprint series have been carefully selected for their contemporary usefulness as well as their historical importance within the intellectual. We reconstruct the book with slight enhancements made for better presentation, without affecting the contents of the original edition.

Most of the works selected for republishing covers a huge range of subjects, from history to anthropology. We believe this reprint edition will be a service to the numerous researchers and practitioners active in this fascinating field. We allow readers to experience the wonder of peering into a scholarly work of the highest order and seminal significance.

MJP Publishers

CONTENTS

Introduction

The Use of Punctuation—Punctuation is a device for marking out the arrangement of a writer's ideas. Reading is thereby made easier than it otherwise would be.

A writer's ideas are expressed by a number of words arranged in groups, the words in one group being more closely connected with one another than they are with those in the next group. An example will show this grouping in its simplest form:

He never convinces the reason, or fills the imagination, or touches the heart.

To understand what is written, the reader must group the words together in the way intended by the writer; and in doing this he can receive assistance in various ways. Partly by the inflection of the words; partly by their arrangement; partly also by punctuation. As to inflection, we see in Latin an adjective and a substantive standing together, yet differing in gender, in number, or in case; and we know that the adjective does not qualify the substantive. But English has not the numerous inflections of Latin. More scrupulous care therefore is needed in the arrangement of words in order to bring together in position such as are connected in meaning. Yet this is not always enough. Except in the very simplest sentences there are generally several arrangements which are grammatically possible; and, though all save one may be absurd in meaning, the reader may waver for a moment before the absurdity strikes him. Some artificial aid is thus needed to prevent him from thinking of any arrangement but the right one. There is no fault, for instance, to be found with the arrangement of the following words, yet, printed without points, they form a mere puzzle:

He had arrived already prepossessed with a strong feeling of the neglect which he had experienced from the Whigs his old friends however all of them appeared ravished to see him offered apologies for the mode in which they had treated him and caught at him as at a twig when they were drowning the influence of his talents they understood and were willing to see it thrown into the opposite scale.

Of course, with a little effort the meaning can be discovered; but if such a little effort had to be put forth in every page of a whole book, reading would become a serious task. By means of points, or "stops," we are spared much of this. The groups are presented ready-made to the eye; and the mind, bent on understanding the thought, is not distracted by having first to discover the connection of the words.

The reader's task is more difficult where two or more ways of grouping the words not only are grammatically possible, but lead each to a more or less intelligible meaning. As a rule he can find out from the context which way the writer meant him to take. One politician writes to another: "I ask you as the recognized leader of our party what you think of this measure;" and nobody accuses the writer of presumption. We might even pass over the following startling sentence without observing the reflection which it casts on a respectable body of men:

Hence he considered marriage with a modern political economist as dangerous.

But when we read that "the State may impose restrictions on the mothers of young children employed in factories," we may well have some doubt whether it is the mothers or the children who are employed in factories. And it would not be easy to give an answer, if we were asked to state the precise meaning of Gray's line:

And all the air a solemn stillness holds.

In longer and more involved sentences the risk of ambiguity is obviously much greater. Now by the judicious use of points ambiguous language can occasionally be made clear. "The mothers-of-young-children employed in factories" is no doubt a bold form, but it leaves us in no doubt as to the meaning. So the ambiguous word "too" does not embarrass us when we read: "This problem, too, easy as it may seem, remains unsolved." (See other examples under Rules XIV. and XV.) Only occasionally, however, can clearness be secured by punctuation. No pointing can help us much in Gray's line, or could have given to Pyrrhus the true reading of "Credo te Æacida Romanos vincere posse." And, even where it would make the meaning clear, it is a lazy device, the over-use of which is the sure sign of careless or unskilful composition. The true remedy for ambiguity is not punctuation, but re-writing.

Punctuation, it is sometimes said, serves to mark the pauses that would be made in speaking. This is so far true; for by the pause we arrange our spoken words into proper groups, thereby enabling our hearers readily to seize the meaning. But between the punctuation of the pen and that of the voice there is a great difference in degree. By the voice we can express the most delicate shades of thought, while only in the roughest way can the comma, the semicolon, and the other points, imitate its effects. As to how far the attempt at imitation should be carried, every writer will have to use his own discretion; but, whether we point freely or sparingly, we must for the reader's sake point consistently. It should at the same time be borne in mind that the lavish use of points often leads to confusion.

General Rules.—Keeping in view the use of punctuation, we can now form two general rules to guide us when we are in doubt which point we should insert, or whether we should insert a point at all.

1. *The point that will keep the passage most free from ambiguity, or make it easiest to read, is the right point to use.*

2. *If the passage be perfectly free from ambiguity and be not less easy to understand without any point, let no point be used.*

The Relativity of Points.—In order to decide in any given case what point ought to be used, we begin by considering the nature of the pause in itself. But we must do more. We must consider how we have pointed the rest of the passage. The pause that should be marked by a comma in one case, may require a semicolon in another case; the colon may take the place that the semicolon would generally fill. This will be best understood by means of the examples that will afterwards be given. (See Rules XXIII., XXV.)

Usage.—Except within somewhat narrow limits, usage does not help us much. Different writers have different methods, and few are consistent. To some extent there is a fair degree of uniformity; for instance, in the placing of colons before quotations, and in the use of inverted commas. But in many cases there can hardly be said to be any fixed usage, and in these we can freely apply the general rules already laid down. Much might be said for a complete disregard of usage, for a thorough recasting of our system of punctuation. Sooner or later something must be done to relieve the overburdened comma of part of the work which it is expected to perform. Not only is the comma a less effective point than it might be, but the habit of using it for so many purposes is exercising a really mischievous effect on English style. In the meantime, and as a step towards a better system, there is an evident advantage in giving to the existing vague usage a more or less precise form. Nothing more than this has been aimed at in the present work.

In giving rules of punctuation we cannot hope to deal with all, or with nearly all, the cases that may arise in writing. Punctuation is intimately connected with style. As forms of thought are infinite in number, so are the modes of expression; and punctuation, adapting itself to these, is an instrument capable of manipulation in a thousand ways. We can therefore set forth only some typical cases, forming a body of examples to which a little reflection will suggest a variety both of applications and of exceptions.

It will be noticed that we do not take the points exactly in their order of strength. It seemed better to deal with the full stop before passing to the punctuation of the parts of a sentence. Again, it may be said that, strictly speaking, italics do not form part of the subject. But they are at any rate so intimately connected with it that to have passed them over would have been merely pedantic. Even the sections on references to notes and on the correction of proofs may not be considered altogether out of place. As few grammatical terms as possible have been made use of. Some have been found necessary in order to secure the brevity of statement proper to a little work on a little subject.

The Full Stop

I. **A full stop is placed at the end of every sentence that is neither exclamatory nor interrogative.**

A penal statute is virtually annulled if the penalties which it imposes are regularly remitted as often as they are incurred. The sovereign was undoubtedly competent to remit penalties without limit. He was, therefore, competent to annul virtually a penal statute. It might seem that there could be no serious objection to his doing formally what he might do virtually.

How much should be put into a sentence is rather a matter of style than of punctuation. The tendency of modern literature is in favour of the short sentence. In the prose of Milton and of Jeremy Taylor, the full stop does not come to release the thought till all the circumstances have been grouped around it, and the necessary qualifications made. In Macaulay the circumstances and the qualifications are set out sentence by sentence. So the steps of reasoning in the example which we have given are stated with that distinct pause between each of them which the reader would make if he thought them out for himself. They might be welded together thus:

Seeing that a penal statute is virtually annulled if the penalties which it imposes are regularly remitted as often as they are incurred, and seeing that the sovereign was undoubtedly competent to remit penalties without limit, it follows that he was competent to annul virtually a penal statute; and it might seem that there could be no serious objection to his doing formally what he might do virtually.

Both forms are correct in point of punctuation. Which is the better form is a question of style. Take another example:

The sides of the mountain were covered with trees; the banks of the brooks were diversified with flowers; every blast shook spices from the rocks; and every mouth dropped fruits upon the ground.

There is here an advantage in putting these four statements together, instead of making four separate sentences. We can more easily combine the details, and so form a single picture—a picture of fertility.

II. **As a rule the full stop is not to be inserted till the sentence be grammatically complete. But some parts of the sentence necessary to make it grammatically complete may be left for the reader to supply.**

It is well said, in every sense, that a man's religion is the chief fact with regard to him. A man's or a nation of men's. By religion I do not mean here the church-creed which he professes, the articles of faith which he will sign and, in words or otherwise, assert. Not this wholly, in many cases not this at all.

III. When a sentence is purposely left unfinished, the dash takes the place of the full stop. (See Rule XL.)

"Excuse me," said I, "but I am a sort of collector." "Not Income-tax?" cried His Majesty, hastily removing his pipe from his lips.

IV. A full stop is placed after most abbreviations, after initial letters, and after ordinal numbers in Roman characters.

Gen. i. 20; two lbs.; A.D. 1883; 3 p.m.; & c., and etc.; M.D., J. S. Mill; William III., King of England; MS., LL.D. (not M.S. and L.L.D.).

Note that the use of the full stop in these cases does not prevent another point from being used immediately after it. But if they occur at the end of a sentence, another full stop is not added; or, more correctly, it may be said that Rule IV. does not apply at the end of a sentence.

"Mr," "Messrs," "Dr"—abbreviations which retain the last letter of the whole word—are written without a point.

The Comma

V. The comma indicates a short pause in a sentence. It is used when we wish to separate words that stand together, and at the same time to stop as little as possible the flow of the sentence.

When the earl reached his own province, he found that preparations had been made to repel him.

Though it is difficult, or almost impossible, to reclaim a savage, bred from his youth to war and the chase, to the restraints and the duties of civilized life, nothing is more easy or common than to find men who have been educated in all the habits and comforts of improved society, willing to exchange them for the wild labours of the hunter and the fisher.

VI. Where there is no danger of obscurity, the subject must not be separated from the predicate by any point.

The eminence of your station gave you a commanding prospect of your duty.

VII. When the subject is long, a comma may be placed after it.

To say that he endured without a murmur the misfortune that now came upon him, is to say only what his previous life would have led us to expect.

In every sentence the subject, whether expressed in one word or in several words, must be grasped as a whole; and, when the subject is long, one is often assisted in doing this by having a point to mark its termination. The eye at once observes the separating line. Note the corresponding pause in the reading of such sentences.

VIII. **When the subject consists of several parts, *e.g.*, of several nouns, a comma is placed after the last part.**

A few daring jests, a brawl, and a fatal stab, make up the life of Marlowe.

Time, money, and friends, were needed to carry on the work.

This rule will appear reasonable if we consider an apparent exception to it. When the last noun sums up all the others, or marks the highest point of a climax, no comma is placed after it.

Freedom, honour, religion was at stake.

If "religion" be regarded as marking the highest point of a climax, the predicate is read with "religion," and with it alone. When so great a thing as religion is said to be at stake, everything else is dropped out of sight, or is held to be included.

But write the three names as if they were of equal importance; the comma should then be inserted:

Freedom, honour, and religion, were at stake.

But it is not necessary to use a point in such a sentence as this: "Time and tide wait for no man." For we see without the aid of a point that the predicate is to be read with the two nouns equally.

The principle might be applied also in cases like the following, though few writers carry it so far:

It was the act of a high-spirited, generous, just nation.

It was the act of a high-spirited, generous, and just, nation.

IX. **Dependent clauses are generally separated from the rest of the sentence in which they occur. The usual point is the comma.**

Be his motives what they may, he must soon disperse his followers.

This relation of your army to the crown will, if I am not greatly mistaken, become a serious dilemma in your politics.

Of course, this rule must be qualified by the rules for the stronger points, especially by those for the semicolon and the colon. It is often necessary to separate the clause from the rest of the sentence by a strong point.

Exceptions

1. No point is needed if either the dependent clause or the principal clause be short.

He would be shocked if he were to know the truth.

But if the dependent clause be inserted parenthetically, it is marked off by commas or the other marks of parenthesis, however short it may be. (See Rule X.)

If the sentence last quoted were inverted, a comma would be placed after the dependent clause.

If he were to know the truth, he would be shocked.

In the first form of this example, "he would be shocked" is a definite, finished statement, the necessary qualification to which should follow with as little pause as possible. But in the inverted form, the first part of the sentence—"if he were to know the truth"—is not a finished statement, and the mind may pause for a moment before going on to the consequence, knowing that the consequence must follow.

2. No point is needed if there be a very close grammatical connection between the dependent clause and some word or words preceding it.

They had so long brooded over their own distresses that they knew nothing of how the world was changing around them.

Note that by the word "so" the clause "that they knew nothing" is joined very closely to the previous part of the sentence; and that the two clauses "that they knew nothing" and "how the world was changing around them," are even more closely joined to one another by the pre[24]position "of." For the same reason, where the object is a clause, there is no point before it.

He confessed to us that he had not thought over the matter.

A useful distinction will afterwards be drawn between the different kinds of relative clauses. (Rule XIV.)

X.   Words thrown in so as to interrupt slightly the flow of a sentence are marked off by commas.

He resolved, therefore, to visit the prisoner early in the morning.

This, I think, is the right view of the case.

The first ideas of beauty formed by the mind are, in all probability, derived from colours.

The following are some of the words and phrases that come under this rule: *therefore, too, indeed, however, moreover, then, accordingly, consequently; in short, in fine,in truth, in fact, to a certain extent, all things considered.*

This rule of high pointing should be applied very sparingly, and might really be restricted to cases like the "I think" of the second example. Nowadays the tendency is against[25] the pointing of such words as "therefore" and "indeed."

Where the words thrown in make a very distinct break in the sentence, they should be pointed off by means of the dash or of brackets.

XI.   **Where two parts of a sentence have some words in common, which are not expressed for each of them, but are given only when the words in which they differ have been separately stated, the second part is marked off by commas.**

His classification is different from, and more comprehensive than, any other which we have met.

This foundation is a nursing-mother of lay, as distinguished from religious, oratorios.

These examples come within the principle of Rule X.

XII.   **When words are common to two or more parts of a sentence, and are expressed only in one part, a comma is often used to show that they are omitted in the other parts.**

London is the capital of England; Paris, of France; Berlin, of Germany.

In the worst volume of elder date, the historian may find something to assist or direct his enquiries; the antiquarian, something to elucidate what requires illustration; the philologist, something to insert in the margin of his dictionary.

Though many writers constantly punctuate contracted sentences in this way, it is well not to insert the comma when the meaning is equally clear without it. It is unnecessary in the following sentence:

Saul hath slain his thousands, and David his ten thousands.

XIII. Words placed out of their natural position in the sentence are often followed by a comma.

1. *The object is usually placed after the verb; when placed at the beginning of the sentence, it should be separated from the subject by a comma, unless the meaning would otherwise be perfectly clear and be readily seized.*

The proportions of belief and of unbelief in the human mind in such cases, no human judgment can determine.

There is the same reason for inserting the comma in such cases as there is for inserting it after a long subject. Moreover, there is often need of some device to remove the ambiguities that are caused by inversion. In English, the meaning of words is so greatly determined by their position that, in altering the usual arrangement of a sentence, there is risk of being misunderstood. The danger of inserting the point in this case is that the object may be read with the words going before, and not with its own verb. If there is a possibility of this, the point should not be used.

Of course no point should be placed after the object in such a sentence as the following:—"One I love, and the other I hate."

> 2. *An adverbial phrase, that is a phrase used as an adverb, is usually placed after the verb; when it begins the sentence, a comma follows it unless it is very short.*

From the ridge a little way to the east, one can easily trace the windings of the river.

In order to gain his point, he did not hesitate to use deception.

In ordinary circumstances I should have acted differently.

No point would be used in the above sentences, if the adverbial phrases occurred in their usual position.

He did not hesitate to use deception in order to gain his point.

Nor is any point used when, as often happens in such sentences, the verb precedes the subject.

Not very far from the foot of the mountain lies the village we hope to reach.

3. *An adjective phrase, that is a phrase used as an adjective, is usually placed immediately after the word which it qualifies; when it appears in any other place, a comma is often usefully placed before it.*

A question was next put to the assembly, of supreme importance at such a moment.

The phrase "of supreme importance at such a moment" is to be taken along with "question"; the comma shows that it is not to be taken along with "assembly." There is here a further reason for the point, inasmuch as the phrase acquires from its position almost the importance of an independent statement. But, where the connexion between the adjective phrase and the substantive is very close, and where there is no risk of ambiguity, no point is to be used. "The morning was come of a mighty day"—such a sentence needs no point. Observe also that co-ordinate adjective phrases take a comma before them, wherever they are placed. (See next rule.)

XIV. Adjective clauses and contracted adjective clauses are marked off by commas, if they are used parenthetically or co-ordinately; no point is used if they are used restrictively[1].

The "Religio Laici," which borrows its title from the "Religio Medici" of Browne, is almost the only

---

1. To distinguish the different kinds of adjective clauses, different names have been used: "co-ordinating" and "restrictive" (Bain); "continuative" and "definitive," or "restrictive" (Mason).

work of Dryden which can be considered as a voluntary effusion.

That sentiment of homely benevolence was worth all the splendid sayings that are recorded of kings.

The advocates for this revolution, not satisfied with exaggerating the vices of their ancient government, strike at the fame of their country itself.

The ships bound on these voyages were not advertised.

Chapter VII., where we stopped reading, is full of interest.

The chapter where we stopped reading is full of interest.

We must explain this distinction at some length; for, on the one hand, it is hardly ever observed, and, on the other hand, almost every sentence that we write furnishes an example of it.

Examine the first sentence which we have quoted. It contains both a co-ordinate clause, "Which borrows its title," &c., and a restrictive clause, "Which can be considered as a voluntary effusion." In distinguishing them we may begin by applying tests of almost a mechanical nature.

 a. The first clause may be thrown into the form of an independent statement; the second cannot. Thus: "The 'Religio Laici' borrows its title from the 'Religio Medici' of Browne. It

is almost the only work," &c.; or, "The 'Religio Laici' (it borrows its title from the 'Religio
Medici' of Browne) is almost the only work,"
&c. We cannot in the same way destroy the
close connexion of the second clause with "the
only work of Dryden."*

b. *The first clause may be omitted and still leave
a complete and intelligent sentence; if we were
to omit the second clause, the sentence would
cease to have any meaning.*

These tests may be practically useful; but they
are rough and by no means infallible. Let us see the
reason for the distinction.

The name "Religio Laici" of itself tells us what
thing is spoken about. It is the name of one thing,
and only of one thing. The clause that follows in-
forms us, indeed, of a fact concerning the poem;
but the information is given purely as information,
not in order to keep us from confounding this "Religio Laici" with some other "Religio Laici" that did
not borrow its title. "Work of Dryden," however, is
the name of a class, for Dryden wrote many works.
Now the whole class is not here in question; it must
be limited, narrowed, or restricted, to one part of
it, namely Dryden's voluntary effusions; and it is
thus limited, narrowed, or restricted, by the relative clause "which can be considered as a voluntary
effusion."

Take another example, where the name in
both cases is that of a class, and note the difference of meaning which results from different

pointing:—"The houses in London which are badly built, ought to be pulled down." "The houses in London" expresses a class of objects; the relative clause limits the name to a smaller class, the badly built houses; and the meaning is, that houses of this smaller class ought to be pulled down. Now insert the comma:—"The houses in London, which are badly built, ought to be pulled down." The class is not narrowed; and the meaning is, that all houses in London, seeing they are badly built, ought to be pulled down.

The difference between the two kinds of relative clauses being understood, there will be no difficulty in applying the rule where an adjective clause is contracted. Compare the fourth example given under the rule with the following sentence:—"People not satisfied with their present condition, should strive to alter it." In this sentence "not satisfied" limits the general name "people"; the advice is given only to one section of the people: the dissatisfied as distinguished from the satisfied people.

So a single adjective may be used co-ordinately:

"What!" replied the Emperor, "you do not see it? It is my star, brilliant."

This is a case where a dash would be more expressive.

Note that the rule applies only where the adjunct immediately follows the substantive. If the adjunct is placed elsewhere, different considerations apply. See Rule XIII.

Neither can any man marvel at the play of puppets, that goeth behind the curtain and adviseth well of the motion.

XV. Words in apposition are generally marked off by commas.

James Watt, the great improver of the steam-engine, died on the 25th of August, 1819.

But where the words in apposition are used in a limiting or distinguishing sense, the principle of Rule XIV. applies, and no point is used. Thus we should write "Burns, the poet," "Dickens, the novelist"; but, if we wished to distinguish them from another Burns and another Dickens, we should omit the comma.

It is of Pliny the naturalist, not of Pliny the letter-writer, that we are now speaking.

Again, where the general name precedes, we should in most cases use no point, for the special name will be restrictive: "the poet Burns," "the novelist Dickens."

There is, perhaps, not much authority for the consistent carrying out of this distinction; but it seems useful and logical. Some cases, such as "Paul the Apostle," "William the Conqueror," "Thomas the Rhymer," "Peter the Hermit," present no difficulty. The name and the descriptive title are blended together, and form as distinctly one name as does "Roderick Random."

XVI. A conjunction marks a transition to something new—enforcing, qualifying, or explaining, what has gone before, and is therefore generally preceded by some point. The proper point before a conjunction is determined by many circumstances: among others, by the more or less close connexion of the things joined, by the number of words, and by the use of points for other purposes in the same sentence. To deal with the different conjunctions one by one, would involve a repetition of much

1. *AND.*—(a) Where "and" joins two single words, as a rule no point is used.

No work has been so much studied and discussed.

Compare this with the following sentence, where groups of words are joined.

The work has been much studied, and has been much discussed.

In the following sentence the insertion of a comma would change the meaning.

On this shelf you will put books and pamphlets published in the present year.

As the sentence stands, "published in the present year" applies both to books and to pamphlets: books published in the present year, and pamphlets published in the present year. If there were a comma before "and," the meaning would be: "On this shelf you will put books of any date, and pamphlets of the present year."

b. When "and" joins the separate words of a series of three or more words, a comma is placed before it.

Trees, and bridges, and houses, were swept down by the flooded stream.

c. But where the different words are intended to be combined quickly, so as to present to the mind only one picture, they would be spoken without any pause, and in writing must not be separated by any point.

Whirling and boiling and roaring like thunder, the stream came down upon them.

d. Two of the words of the series may be more closely connected with one another than with the other words of the series, and are, therefore, not to be separated by any point.

In the following sentence, "all" qualifies both "tracts" and "pamphlets," and thus joins them closely.

My unbound books, and all my tracts and pamphlets, are to be tied up with pink tape.

e. When "and" occurs only between the two last words of the series, the comma is usually inserted before it.

Trumpets, drums, and kettle-drums, contended in noise with the shouts of a numerous rabble.

Many writers omit this comma. But it seems useful in order to make the previous rule (*d*) effective.

2. When "and" joins two phrases, a comma generally precedes it.

The ceremony was performed in the accustomed manner, and with due solemnity.

If, as in the following sentence, a preposition is common to two phrases, and is not repeated in the second, no comma is used.

With proper care and good instruments, the work may be successfully carried out.

3. When "and" joins two clauses, the preceding point may be the comma, the semicolon, or even the full stop. Which point is right in any particular case, will depend upon considerations set out in other rules.

The following example illustrates different cases:

Within that charmed rock, so Torridge boatmen tell, sleeps now the old Norse Viking in his leaden coffin, with all his fairy treasure and his crown of gold; and, as the boy looks at the spot, he fancies, and almost hopes, that the day may come when he shall have to do his duty against the invader as boldly as the men of Devon did then. And past him, far below, upon the soft south-eastern breeze, the stately ships go sliding out to sea.

OR

The rules for the conjunction "and" apply with little change to the conjunction "or"; but there are one or two special points to note.

a. When "or" is preceded at no great distance by "either" or "whether," the two words should be separated by no point.

They must either yield this point or resign.

It does not matter whether we go or stay.

But a point is inserted if the words stand farther apart, or if each is followed by a complete clause.

Either this road leads to the town, or we have misunderstood the directions.

b. "Or," joining two alternatives, takes no point before it; but when it joins two words that are used, not as real alternatives, but as synonyms, a comma is inserted.

England or France might be asked to join the alliance.

Here "or" is used as a real alternative conjecture, and therefore without any point. In the following examples, the "or" joins equivalent expressions:

England, or the nation of shopkeepers, would never be asked to join such an alliance.

We perceive, or are conscious of, nothing but changes, or events.

As a reason for the insertion of the comma in these two examples, it may be said that the repetition of an idea already expressed does for a moment stop the flow of the sentence. A real alternative, on the other hand, forms an essential part of it, and is within its current.

XVII. **In cases where no point would be used before a conjunction, a comma is inserted if the conjunction be omitted.**

I pay this tribute to the memory of that noble, reverend, learned, excellent person.

In the following examples no point occurs; for it cannot be said that a conjunction is omitted. To insert the conjunction would be to express a slightly different shade of meaning:

A grand old man.

Three tall young soldiers.

"Old man" is virtually a single word and in fact many languages use only a single word to express the idea.

XVIII. **Where a comma would be used if the conjunction were expressed, some stronger point may be used if it be omitted.**

Let us get an American revenue as we have got an American Empire. English privileges have made it all that it is; English privileges alone will make it all that it can be.

XIX. **A comma is placed after a noun or a pronoun in the vocative case, if a mark of exclamation be not used, or be reserved till the first distinct pause in the sentence.**

Yet I own, my lord, that yours is not an uncommon character.

I am, Sir, yours truly, John Smith.

O Italy, gather thy blood into thy heart!

O Thou, who in the heavens dost dwell!

Whether a comma or a mark of exclamation ought to be used after the vocative case, depends entirely on the degree of emphasis with which the words would be spoken. If, in speaking, a slight pause would be made, the comma, not the mark of exclamation, is the proper point.

XX. **If a word be repeated in order to give it intensive force, a comma follows it each time that it occurs; but, in the case of an adjective repeated before a noun, not after the last expression of it.**

It was work, work, work, from morning till night.

He travelled a long, long way.

Dean Alford, in "The Queen's English," says that this mode of pointing such expressions as "the wide wide world," "the deep deep sea," makes them absolute nonsense. The suggestion of a pause seems to us to bring out more effectively the intensive force of the repetition. And we doubt whether Dean Alford himself would have omitted the comma in our first example.

The Semicolon

XXI. The semicolon is the point usually employed to separate parts of a sentence between which there is a very distinct break, but which are too intimately connected to be made separate sentences.

The patient dates his pleasure from the day when he feels that his cure has begun; and, perhaps, the day of his perfect re-establishment does not yield him pleasure so great.

The author himself is the best judge of his own performance; no one has so deeply meditated on the subject; no one is so sincerely interested in the event.

Not one word is said, nor one suggestion made, of a general right to choose our own governors; to cashier them for misconduct; and to form a government for ourselves.

The semicolon is used in enumerations, as in the last example, in order to keep the parts more distinctly separate.

XXII. When a sentence consists of two or more independent clauses not joined by conjunctions, the clauses are separated by semicolons.

To command a crime is to commit one; he who commands an assassination, is by every one regarded as an assassin.

His knowledge was too multifarious to be always exact; his pursuits were too eager to be always cautious.

If the conjunction "and" were inserted in the last sentence, the comma would be used instead of the semicolon. A conjunction forms a bridge over the gap between two statements, and, where they are neither long nor complicated, we pass from one to the other without noticing any distinct break. But there is such a break when the conjunction is omitted, and therefore we use a stronger point. The two parts of an antithesis are generally separated in this way.

XXIII. A pause generally indicated by a comma may be indicated by a semicolon when commas are used in the sentence for[45] other purposes. (See *Introduction: Relativity of Points*.)

I got several things of less value, but not all less useful to me, which I omitted setting down before: as, in particular, pens, ink, and paper; several parcels in the captain's, mate's, gunner's, and carpenter's keeping; three or four compasses, some mathematical instruments, dials, perspectives, charts, and books of navigation.

In this I was certainly in the wrong too, the honest, grateful creature having no thought but what consisted of the best principles, both as a religious Christian and as a grateful friend; as appeared afterward to my full satisfaction.

In the first sentence the semicolon enables us to group the objects enumerated. Had commas been used throughout, the reader would have been left to find out the arrangement for himself.

The Colon

XXIV. The colon is used to indicate pauses more abrupt than those indicated by the semicolon.

God has willed it: submit in thankfulness.

The wind raged, and the rain beat against the window: it was a miserable day.

Nevertheless, you will say that there must be a difference between true poetry and true speech not poetical: what is the difference?

The first example contains two clauses that are connected in such a way as to justify us in putting them into one sentence; that it is God's will, is a reason for submitting. The proper point therefore should be something less than the full stop. But there is a striking difference between the clauses; for we pass from an affirmation to a command. Therefore something more than the semicolon is needed. Had the clauses been similar in construction, the pause would have been sufficiently indicated by the semicolon: "God has willed it; man has resisted."

In the second example there is not the same change of grammatical construction, but the change in thought is equally great; we pass from a statement of details to a statement of the general result. The colon is frequently used in sentences of this kind, where the phrase "in short" is implied but is not expressed.

Many writers indicate such abrupt changes by means of the dash.

XXV. **A pause generally indicated by a semi-colon may be indicated by a colon, when the semicolon is used in the sentence for pauses of a different nature.**

The "Essay" plainly appears the fabric of a poet: what Bolingbroke supplied could be only the first principles; the order, illustration, and embellishments, must all be Pope's.

Not that we are to think that Homer wanted judgment, because Virgil had it in a more eminent degree; or that Virgil wanted invention, because Homer possessed a larger share of it: each of these great authors had more of both than, perhaps, any man besides, and are only said to have less in comparison with one another.

Homer hurries and transports us with a commanding impetuosity; Virgil leads us with an attractive majesty: Homer scatters with a generous profusion; Virgil bestows with a careful magnificence.

Compare these examples with those given to show how the semicolon replaces the comma. (Rule XXIII.) Note also how the last sentence is divided in the middle into two parts, and that each of these two parts is itself divided into two parts. By Rule XXII. the second division is indicated by the semicolon; and we bring out the grouping of the sentence by using a colon for the first division.

XXVI. The colon is used before enumerations, especially where "namely," or "viz.," is implied but is not expressed; and when so used it is sometimes followed by the dash.

Three nations adopted this law: England, France, and Germany.

One thing thou lackest: go thy way, sell whatsoever thou hast, and give to the poor.

Dr Johnson's chief works are the following:—"Rasselas," The Dictionary, "The Lives of the Poets," and "The Vanity of Human Wishes."

When, as in the last example, a list of things is given in a formal way, the dash is generally added. The combination of the two points is partly an attempt to find a point stronger than the colon and not so strong as the full stop, partly, perhaps, an imitation of a finger-post.

XXVII. The colon is generally placed before a quotation, when notice of the quo-

tation is given by some introductory words. In this case also the dash is sometimes used.

In this passage exception may fairly be taken to one short sentence, that in which he says: "The law ought to forbid it, because conscience does not permit it."

On the last morning of his life he wrote these words:—"I have named none to their disadvantage. I thank God He hath supported me wonderfully."

The colon and the dash are used together where the quotation is introduced by formal words such as the following:—"He spoke these words," "he spoke as follows," "he made this speech." But, in the first sentence quoted above, the introductory words are grammatically[50] incomplete without the quotation, which forms the object of the verb "says"; the colon accordingly is the strongest point that can be used. Sometimes the connexion between the introductory words and the quotation may be so close, or the quotation itself may be so short, as to make the comma sufficient.

He kept repeating to us, "The world has sadly changed."

Short phrases quoted in the course of the sentence need not have any point before them.

It was a usual saying of his own, that he had "no genius for friendship."

XXVIII. The colon may be placed after such words and phrases as the following, when used in marking a new stage in an argument:—Again, further, to proceed, to sum up, to resume.

To sum up: If you will conform to the conditions I have mentioned, I will sign the agreement.

But to bring this sermon to its proper conclusion: If Astrea, or Justice, never finally took her leave of the world till the day that, &c.

After these words, we have a choice of[51] the comma, the colon, and the full stop. The comma will generally be used if the argument be contained in a single sentence; the full stop, if the argument be of very considerable length.

The Point of Interrogation

XXIX.   The point of interrogation is placed after a direct question.

Where are you going, my pretty maid?

Whether of them twain did the will of his father?

The question may end in the middle of a sentence:

Is he happy? you ask.

We have sometimes the choice of putting the point of interrogation in the middle or at the end of the sentence.

You would not consent to that, by whomsoever proposed.

You would not consent to that?—by whomsoever proposed.

There is a slight shade of difference in meaning; in the second form, "by whomsoever proposed" is added as an afterthought.

XXX. Indirect questions are not strictly questions at all, and therefore should not be followed by a point of interrogation.

He asked me whether I had seen his friend; whether I had spoken to him; and how I liked him.

If we restore these questions to the direct form, the point of interrogation is inserted.

He asked me: "Have you seen my friend? Have you spoken to him? How do you like him?"

XXXI. When a sentence contains more than one question, sometimes the point of interrogation is placed after each of them, sometimes it is placed only at the end of the sentence. It is placed after each, if each is in reality a distinct question; it is placed only at the end, if the separate questions so unite as to need but a single answer.

In many cases it will be a matter of individual taste to say whether they do so unite.

Is it better that estates should be held by those who have no duty than by those who have one? by those whose character and destination point to virtues than by those who have no rule and direction in the expenditure of their estates but their own will and appetite?

Do you imagine that it is the Land Tax Act which raises your revenue, that it is the annual vote in the Committee of Supply which gives you your army, or that it is the Mutiny Bill which inspires it with bravery and discipline? No! surely no!

Oh! why should Hymen ever blightThe roses Cupid wore?Or why should it be ever nightWhere it was day before?Or why should women have a tongue,Or why should it be cursed,In being, like my Second, long,And louder than my First?

XXXII. Exclamations in an interrogative form take a mark of exclamation after them, not a point of interrogation. (See Rule XXXV.)

XXXIII. A point of interrogation enclosed within brackets is sometimes used to indicate that there is a doubt whether the statement preceding it is true, or whether the expression preceding it is well applied, or that some statement or expression is made or used ironically.

While you are revelling in the delights (?) of the London season, I am leading a hermit life, with no companions save my books.

The Mark of Exclamation

XXXIV. The mark of exclamation is placed after interjections and words used interjectionally; that is to say, after expressions of an exclamatory nature. The exclamation may be one of surprise or of fear, or the utterance of a wish, a command, or a prayer.

Quick! Begone! Out of my sight!

Heaven preserve us!

Would that better feelings moved them!

O Lord, be merciful unto me, a sinner!

Interjections are not always followed immediately, and are sometimes not allowed at all, by a mark of exclamation. No rule can be given more precise than this:

1. That we should not insert a mark of exclamation immediately after an interjection, unless we should make a distinct pause after it in speaking; and

2. that no mark of exclamation is to be used at all, unless the exclamatory nature of the sentence is more or less strongly marked. It is useful to notice the difference between "O" and "Oh." The former is used only before the vocative case, and never has a mark of exclamation, or indeed any point, placed immediately after it.

Alas! all our hopes are blasted.Lo, he cometh!O Dido, Dido, most unhappy Dido!Unhappy wife, still more unhappy widow! Oh, do not reckon that old debt to my account to-day!

XXXV. The mark of exclamation is placed after sentences which, though interrogatory in form, are really exclamatory.

How could he have been so foolish!

And shall he never see an end to this state of things! Shall he never have the due reward of labour! Shall unsparing taxation never cease to make him a miserable dejected being, a creature famishing in the midst of abundance, fainting, expiring with hunger's feeble moan, surrounded by a carolling creation!

This rule might be put in another way by saying that a mark of exclamation, and not a point of interrogation, is placed after what are called rhetorical questions, or statements made more striking by being put in the form of questions. They are not asked for the sake of receiving a direct answer, and are in reality exclamations. Still all rhetorical questions are not thus punctuated; the point of interrogation is sometimes more effective. The sentences quoted under Rule XXXI. would lose much of their force if marks of exclamation were used. In each case we must decide whether the sentence strikes us most as a question or as the expression of emotion.

XXXVI. The mark of exclamation is sometimes placed after an ironical statement.

They did not fight, tens against thousands; they did not fight for wives and children, but for lands and plunder: therefore they are heroes!

The mark of exclamation keeps up the semblance of seriousness which is of the essence of irony.

XXXVII. The mark of exclamation is placed after the statement of some absurdity.

He has been labouring to prove that Shakespeare's plays were written by Bacon!

To him the parliamentary vote was a panacea for all human ills, and the ballot-box an object as sacred as the Holy Grail to a knight of the Round Table!

The same reason applies to its use after such sentences as after ironical statements.

XXXVIII. The mark of exclamation may be placed after any impressive or striking thought.

The Angel of Death has been abroad throughout the land: you may almost hear the very beating of his wings!

It may be doubted whether the mark of exclamation is in such cases of any great service; for the impressiveness of a sentence ought to appear in the sentence itself, or to be given to it by the context. There is a real danger, as the style of many people shows, in thinking that punctuation is intended to save the trouble of careful composition. In putting the mark after pure exclamations, usage is more or less uniform; with regard to impressive sentences, we are left entirely to our own discretion.

XXXIX. When a sentence contains more than one exclamation, sometimes the mark of exclamation is placed only after the last, sometimes it is placed after each of them, the test being whether or not they are in reality, as well as in form, several exclamations. (Compare Rule XXXI.)

Though all are thus satisfied with the dispensations of Nature, how few listen to her voice! how few follow her as a guide!

What a mighty work he has thus brought to a successful end, with what perseverance, what energy, with what fruitfulness of resource!

The Dash

XL. The chief purpose of the dash is to indicate that something is left unfinished. Accordingly, it marks a sudden, or abrupt, change in the grammatical structure of a sentence.

When I remember how we have worked together, and together borne misfortune; when I remember—but what avails it to remember?

And all this long story was about—what do you think?

"We cannot hope to succeed, unless——" "But we must succeed."

Note that it is the long dash that is used at the end of a sentence.

The full stop is not added where the dash marks an unfinished sentence. But it is common to add the point of interrogation or the mark of exclamation.

XLI. The dash is used to mark a faltering or hesitating speech.

Well—I don't know—that is—no, I cannot accept it.

XLII. An unexpected turn of the thought may be marked by the dash.

He entereth smiling and—embarrassed. He holdeth out his hand to you to shake, and—draweth it back again. He casually looketh in about dinner-time— when the table is full. He offereth to go away, seeing you have company—but is induced to stay.

French history tends naturally to memoirs and anecdotes, in which there is no improvement to desire but that they were—true.

XLIII. When the subject of a sentence is of such length, or of such complexity, that its connexion with the verb might easily be lost sight of, it is sometimes left hanging in the sentence, and its place supplied by some short expression that sums it up. A dash follows the subject when thus abandoned.

Physical Science, including Chemistry, Geology, Geography, Astronomy; Metaphysics, Philology, Theology; Economics, including Taxation and Finance; Politics and General Literature—all occupied by turn, and almost simultaneously, his incessantly active mind.

The colon is sometimes used in such cases; but the dash seems preferable, as it is the point that marks a change in the structure of a sentence.

XLIV. The dash is sometimes used instead of brackets before and after a parenthesis.

This was amongst the strongest pledges for thy truth, that never once—no, not for a moment of weakness—didst thou revel in the vision of coronets and honour from man.

XLV. The dash is sometimes used instead of the colon, where the word "namely" is implied, but is not expressed.

The most extreme example of such theories is perhaps to be found in the attempt to distribute all law under the two great commandments—love to God, and love to one's neighbour.

In this sentence, however, the colon is preferable. (See Rule XXVI.). The dash should be used for this purpose only when it is necessary to use the colon in the same sentence for other purposes.

XLVI. The dash is used in rhetorical repetition; for instance, where one part of the sentence, such as the subject, is repeated at intervals throughout the sentence, and the rest of the sentence is kept suspended.

Cannot you, in England—cannot you, at this time of day—cannot you, a House of Commons, trust to the principle which has raised so mighty a revenue?

XLVII. A dash following a full stop occurs between the side-heading of a paragraph and the paragraph itself.

Extent and Boundaries.—England (including Wales) is bounded on the north by Scotland; on the west by the Irish Sea, St George's Channel, and the Atlantic Ocean; on the south by the English Channel; and on the east by the German Ocean.

XLVIII. **When we place after a quotation the name of the author from whom it is taken, the full stop and the dash are used in the same way.**

"One touch of nature makes the whole word kin."—*Shakespeare.*

XLIX. **The dash is sometimes used in place of, or in addition to, other points, in order to indicate a pause greater than usual.**

Now where is the revenue which is to do all these mighty things? Five-sixths repealed—abandoned-sunk—gone—lost for ever.

The highest rank;—a splendid fortune;—and a name, glorious till it was yours,—were sufficient to have supported you with meaner abilities than I think you possess.

There is seldom any reason for the use of double points. In the last example they cannot be said to be of any real service. But the dash may sometimes be rightly employed in addition to the full stop, in order to mark a division of discourse midway between the sentence and the paragraph. Even Cobbett, who abhors the dash, permits it to be used for this purpose. The report of a conversation is often printed in this way.

Brackets (or The Parenthesis)

L. When a clause not strictly belonging to a sentence is thrown in, so to speak, in passing, the clause is enclosed within brackets.

It seems better to use the term "brackets" both for the curved and for the square brackets. "Parenthesis" can then be kept to its proper use, as the name for the words themselves which form the break in the sentence. We may note that in like manner the terms "comma," "colon," "semicolon," originally signified divisions of a sentence, not marks denoting the divisions. "Period" meant a complete sentence; and it still retains the meaning, somewhat specialized.

It is said, because the priests are paid by the people (the pay is four shillings per family yearly), therefore they object to their leaving.

In full confidence of this unalterable truth, I now (*quod felix faustumque sit*) lay the first stone of the Temple of Peace.

Over and above the enclosing brackets, a parenthesis causes no change in the punctuation of the sentence that contains it; in other words, if we were to omit the parenthesis, no change ought to be necessary in the punctuation of the rest of the sentence. The comma is inserted after the parenthesis in the first example, because the comma would be needed even if there were no parenthesis.

In the second example, there would be no comma before "lay," if there were no parenthesis; accordingly the comma is not to be inserted merely because there is a parenthesis. A parenthesis is sufficiently marked off by brackets.

Observe also that the comma in the first example is placed after, not before, the parenthesis. The reason for this is that the parenthesis belongs to the first part of the sentence, not to the second.

LI. A complete sentence occurring parenthetically in a paragraph is sometimes placed within brackets.

Godfrey knew all this, and felt it with the greater force because he had constantly suffered annoyance from witnessing his father's sudden fits of unrelentingness, for which his own habitual irresolution[68] deprived him of all sympathy. (He was not critical on the faulty indulgence which preceded these fits; *that* seemed to him natural enough.) Still there was just the chance, Godfrey thought, that his father's pride might see this marriage in a light that would induce him to hush it up, rather than turn his son out and make the family the talk of the country for ten miles round.

Note that the full stop should be placed inside, not outside, the brackets.

LII. Where, in quoting a passage, we throw in parenthetically something of our own, we may use square brackets.

Compare the following account of Lord Palmerston: "I have heard him [Lord Palmerston] say that he occasionally found that they [foreign ministers] had been deceived by the open manner in which he told them the truth."

"The *Leviathan* of Hobbes, a work now-a-days but little known [and not better known now than in Bentham's time], and detested through prejudice, and at second-hand, as a defence of despotism, is an attempt to base all political society upon a pretended contract between the people and the sovereign."—*Principles of Legislation*.

To use the square brackets in this way is often more convenient than to break the inverted commas and to begin them again. But in the case of the word *sic*—where it is inserted in a quotation to point out that the word preceding it is rightly quoted, and is not inserted by mistake—the ordinary brackets are used.

"The number of inhabitants were (*sic*) not more than four millions."

Another case may be mentioned in which the square brackets are used: where in the passage quoted some words have been lost, and are filled in by conjecture. Prof. Stubbs quotes from one of the Anglo-Saxon laws:

"If ceorls have a common meadow, or other partible land to fence, and some have fenced their part, some have not, and [strange cattle come in and] eat up the common corn or grass, let those go who own the gap and compensate to the others."

Inverted Commas

LIII. When we quote without any change the words of another person, they are enclosed within inverted commas. If they are quoted in the indirect form, or if we quote merely the substance, and neglect the exact words, inverted commas are not used.

Thereupon the mob bursts in and inquires, "What are you doing for the people?"

Thereupon the mob bursts in and inquires what you are doing for the people.

He says: "There is no property of any description, if it be rightfully held, which had not its foundation in labour."

He frequently calls them "absurd," and applies to them such epithets as "jargon," "fustian," and the like.

The last sentence might be written without inverted commas. By using them we call special attention to the fact that these were the words actually employed, and are not simply words like them.

So, in a passage quoted in the indirect form, if part be quoted exactly, it is placed within inverted commas.

The Duke of Portland warmly approved of the work, but justly remarked that the king was not "so absolute a thing of straw" as he was represented in it.

Words referred to simply as words are either placed within inverted commas or put in italics.

The word "friendship," in the sense we commonly mean by it, is not so much as named in the New Testament.

LIV. When a quotation is interrupted, as in the report of a conversation, each continuous part of the quotation is enclosed within inverted commas.

"Pardon me, madam," answered Henry, "it was of one Silas Morton I spoke."

LV. When a quotation occurs in another quotation, single inverted commas are used for the former.

"What have you done?" said one of Balfour's brother officers. "My duty," said Balfour firmly. "Is it not written, 'Thou shalt be zealous even to slaying'?"

Some writers use the single commas in ordinary cases. For the inner quotation they would then use the double commas.

LVI. **A word that is not classical English, or is used in a sense in which it is not classical English, is either enclosed within inverted commas or italicized.**

Those that have "located" (*located*) previous to this period are left in undisputed possession, provided they have improved the land.

Before long, Beckey received not only "the best" foreigners (as the phrase is in our noble and admirable society slang), but some of "the best" English people too.

Foreign words are always italicized. (Rule LXIV.)

LVII. **The titles of books, of essays, and of other compositions; the names of periodicals; and the names of ships, are either enclosed within inverted commas or italicized.**

In these "Miscellanies" was first published the "Art of Sinking in Poetry," which, by such a train of consequences as usually passes in literary quarrels, gave in a short time, according to Pope's account, occasion to the "Dunciad."

The "Emily St Pierre" (or *Emily St Pierre*), a British ship, was captured on the 18th March, 1862.

It appeared in the "London Gazette" (or *London Gazette*).

The names of periodicals and of ships are more often written in italics than enclosed within inverted commas.

LVIII. If a quotation contains a question, the point of interrogation stands within the inverted commas.

In a voice which was fascination itself, the being addressed me, saying, "Wilt thou come with me? Wilt thou be mine?"

LIX. If an interrogative sentence ends with a quotation, the point of interrogation stands outside the inverted commas.

What does this honourable person mean by "a tempest that outrides the wind"?

Observe how in the example given under Rule LV. the point of interrogation stands within the double inverted commas, but outside the single inverted commas.

LX. If an interrogative sentence ends with a quotation which is itself interrogatory, the point of interrogation is placed outside the inverted commas.

Hast thou never cried, "What must I do to be saved"?

The reason is, that the question to be answered is not the quoted question, but "hast thou never cried?" No writer has been bold enough to insert two points of interrogation.

LXI. **The last three rules apply also to exclamatory sentences.**

    1. But I boldly cried out, "Woe unto this city!"

    2. Alas, how few of them can say, "I have striven to the very utmost"!

    3. How fearful was the cry: "Help, or we perish"!

LXII. **Where an interrogative sentence ends with a quotation of an exclamatory nature, or an exclamatory sentence ends with a quotation of an interrogative nature, it seems better to place at the end both the point of interrogation and the mark of exclamation, the one inside, the other outside, the inverted commas.**

Do you remember who it was that wrote

    "Whatever England's fields display,The fairest scenes are thine, Torbay!"?

    How much better to cease asking the question, "What would he have done in different circumstances?"!

    Where inverted commas are not used, it seems sufficient to have only one point, which must be the one required by the whole sentence, not by the quotation.

Do you remember the passage where Burke alludes to the old warning of the Church—*Sursum corda?*

Italics

LXIII. Words to be specially emphasized may be put in italics. In writing, the substitute for italics is underlining.

What, it may well be asked, can the interests of the community be those of—I do not say *an* individual, but—*the* individual?

The voice can unmistakably indicate what are the emphatic words; but italics, only a feeble substitute, ought not to be used unless every other means of emphasizing fail. Many writers of authority have strongly, and very justly, condemned the too frequent use of them.

Double underlining in letter-writing need not be here adverted to. If the person to whom one writes a letter is likely to read it without appreciation or care, one is entitled to adopt any means that will ensure attention. But if double underlining is allowable only on this ground, general rules are obviously of no use.

LXIV. Words from a foreign language which have not become classical English words, are written in italics.

The slightest *double entendre* made him blush to the eyes.

Knowledge of French is a *sine quâ non*.

When foreign words become English, they are no longer italicized. Among such words are: rationale, aide-de-camp, quartette, naïve, libretto. It is often a matter of discretion to say whether a word is so far naturalized that it should be written in the ordinary way.

LXV. Names of newspapers and magazines, and names of ships, are generally written in italics; as the *Times*, the *Fort-nightly Review*, the *Great Eastern*.

The Hyphen

LXVI. The hyphen is used between the component parts of some compound words.

Paper-knife; book-keeping; coal-pit; water-carrier; printing-press; sea-water; man-of-war; now-a-days; high-art decoration; good-looking.

There is no rule to distinguish the compound words that take a hyphen from those that do not. If one be in doubt about a particular word, the best thing to do is to refer to a dictionary.

LXVII. When one syllable of a word ends with a vowel, and the next syllable begins with the same vowel, the hyphen is placed between the syllables to indicate that the two vowels do not form a diphthong, that is, that they should not be pronounced together.

Co-operative; co-ordinate; pre-eminently; re-establish; re-echo.

In the same way the hyphen sometimes ensures that two consonants shall be pronounced separately; as in "book-keeping," "shell-less," "cock-crow," "sword-dance."

LXVIII. **As a rule, a hyphen should not be placed after a simple prefix: "contravene," "preternatural," "hypercritical," "bilateral."**

To this there are some exceptions:

a.   "Anti-religious," "ultra-liberal," "semi-lunar," "co-eval." In these words the pronunciation is more clearly marked by inserting the hyphen. Compare "antiseptic," "antinomian," "ultramontane," "semicircle."

Perhaps among these exceptions should also be included such words as "pseudo-critic," "non-ego," "non-existent." Compare "pseudonym," where the prefix is contracted, and "nonentity." Words like "pre-eminent," divided for the same reason, have already been noted.

b.   "Re-creation," "re-mark." The hyphen distinguishes the etymological meaning of these words as distinguished from their derived and ordinary meaning.

c.   "Pre-Norman," "anti-Darwinian," "philo-Turk." If the capital-letter be retained where a prefix is put to a proper name, the hyphen is obviously necessary.

LXIX. When a number is written in words and not in figures, the words making up the number, if there be more words than one, are in certain cases separated from each other by the hyphen.

The numbers to which this rule applies are the cardinal and the ordinal numbers from twenty-one and twenty-first to ninety-nine and ninety-ninth inclusive. The hyphen is used also when the words are inverted; as "four-and-thirty," "six-and-fortieth."

LXX. Fractional parts written in words are separated in the same way, a hyphen being placed between the numerator and denominator; as "two-thirds," "three-sixteenths."

But if the word "part" or the word "share" follows, the hyphen is not used; as "two third parts."

LXXI. Several words may be joined by hyphens, in order to indicate that they are to be read together.

The I-believe-of-Eastern-derivation monosyllable "Bosh."

Additional restrictions were advocated in the cases of mothers-of-young-children employed in factories.

As this last sentence stands, the hyphen is really the only means of making it perfectly clear that those who are referred to as employed in factories are the mothers, not the children. Hyphens are sometimes used in cases like the following: "A never-to-be-forgotten event," "peace-at-any-rate principles." They are almost invariably used in "well-to-do," "alack-a-day."

LXXII. The prefix "a" before the gerund is followed by a hyphen.

They went a-hunting.

I lay a-thinking.

Note that "agoing" is not divided.

LXXIII.   When a word is divided at the end of a line, part of the word being in the next line, a hyphen is placed after the part at the end of the line.

So far as rules can be given for the division of the word, it may be said:

a.   The division must be at the end of a syllable. The syllable according to etymological derivation, and the syllable according to pronunciation, are not always the same. In case of conflict the pronunciation is to be the guide.

b.   The part in the next line should, if possible, begin with a consonant. An examination of a number of words will show that this is only another way of saying that we should be guided by pronunciation.

c. Double letters are divided; as "at-tract," "profes-sion," "dif-ficulty."

The following examples are given consecutively from a book taken at random. This seems the best way of illustrating the rule:

Con-fidently; investi-gated; some-thing; in-stitu-tion; diffi-culty; at-tractions; exclu-sively; kins-man; self-organized; en-tangled; col-lective; intermis-sion; ma-terials; chan-cellor; col-legc; in-dus-trious; sub-ject; his-tory; con-dition; Low-land-ers; or-ganization; re-cognized; in-famous.

Some selected examples may be also given:

Resem-blance; hum-ble; se-cond; trans-lator; justifi-able; east-ern; endea-vour.

The Apostrophe

LXXIV. The apostrophe is used to indicate that some letter or letters of a word are left out.

"E'er" for "ever," "can't" for "cannot," "don't" for "do not," "'gin" for "begin."

The apostrophe is not used when the word, though contracted in the middle, retains its original pronunciation; as "Dr." or "Mr." But it is used where the contraction is at the end of the word: "tho'," "Peterboro'."

LXXV. The apostrophe marks the possessive case of nouns. The following rules determine where it is to be placed:

Nouns in the singular number—

1. **The letter "s" is added, and the apostrophe is placed before it.**

The king's abode. A patriot's reward.

2. **If the** *nominative singular of the noun ends in "s," another "s" is not added if the repetition*

of hissing sounds would be displeasing to the ear. The apostrophe is then placed at the end of the word.

Hercules' club. Augustus' dignity.

Words of one syllable follow the first rule: "James's share." Some words of two syllables follow the first rule, some the second: "the princess's birthday"; "Francis' style."

This distinction is sanctioned by usage. But it may judiciously be disregarded. In speaking we almost entirely ignore it. Why should we trouble ourselves with it in writing?

Nouns in the plural number—

1. **The apostrophe is placed after the "s" of the plural.**

Boys' clothing. Our friends' troubles.

2. *If* **the plural do not end in "s," an "s" is added,** *and the apostrophe is placed before it.*

Men's opinions. The children's pleasure.

LXXVI. The apostrophe is used before the "s" of the plural when single letters are used as words.

Mind your p's and q's.

He does not dot his i's nor cross his t's.

Marks of Ellipsis

LXXVII. When, in the middle of a quotation, a part is omitted, several asterisks or several full stops are placed in a line to mark the omission.

Clarendon makes the following remark about Lord Falkland: "Yet two things he could never bring himself to whilst he continued in that office, that was to his death; for which he was contented to be reproached as for omissions in a most necessary part of his place. The one, employing of spies, or giving any countenance or entertainment to them. * * * The other, the liberty of opening letters, upon a suspicion that they might contain matter of a dangerous consequence." (One sentence omitted.)

"The French and Spanish nations," said Louis XIV., "are so united that they will henceforth be only one.... My grandson, at the head of the Spaniards, will defend the French. I, at the head of the French, will defend the Spaniards."

"He who in former years," wrote Horace Walpole of his father, "was asleep as soon as his head touched the pillow ... now never sleeps above an hour without waking."

If the passage omitted be of very considerable length, for instance if it be a complete paragraph, or if a line of poetry be omitted, the asterisks are placed in a line by themselves. There is a tendency to confine the asterisk to such cases, and to use the full stop for shorter ellipses. If a complete sentence be omitted, the number of additional full stops is generally four; if a passage be omitted in the middle of a sentence, the number is generally three.

When some of the letters of a name are omitted, their place is supplied by a line or dash, whose length depends on the number of letters omitted.

The scene of our story is laid in the town of B———. There was one H———, who, I learned in after days, was seen expiating some maturer offence in the hulks.

Blakesmoor in H———shire.

References to Notes

Notes are generally placed at the foot of a page; though sometimes they are collected at the end of a chapter, or even at the end of a book. Various devices are in use for indicating the passage in the text to which a note refers.

1. The six reference signs: the "asterisk" (*), the "dagger" (†) (also called the "obelisk"), the "double dagger" (‡), the "section" (§), the "parallels" (||), the "paragraph" (¶). They are suitable only where the notes are placed at the foot of a page, and are invariably used in the order in which we have mentioned them.

If the number of notes in one page exceeds six, the signs are doubled. The seventh note is marked thus: **; the eighth, ††; the ninth, ‡‡; and so on. But it is better, in cases where the notes are so numerous, to **use** other means of reference.

2. Figures: either within parentheses, as (1), (2), (3), &c.; or, more usually, printed in the raised or "superior" form, as [1] [2] [3], &c. Sometimes the first note in each page is

marked;[1] but it is now common, in books divided into chapters, to mark the first note in each chapter with [1] and then go on with continuous numbers to the end of the chapter.

"Superior" figures are now the most usual marks of reference in English books.

3. Letters; which also may either be placed within parentheses or be printed in "superior" form: (a), (b), (c), &c., or [a] [b] [c], &c. Italic letters are sometimes used. As a rule the first note in each page is marked (a) or [a]. If in one page there are more notes than there are letters in the alphabet (which sometimes happens), we go to (aa), (bb), (cc), &c., [aa] [bb] [cc]. The letter "j" is often omitted.

It is less common to make the letters continuous from page to page.

The sign, whatever it may be, is placed at the beginning of the note, and also in the text immediately after the part to which the note refers. The note may refer to a whole sentence, to a part of a sentence, even to a single word; the sign is placed as the case may be, at the end of the sentence, at the end of the part referred to, or after the single word.

How to Correct a Printer's Proof

EXPLANATION

1. Where a word is to be changed from small let-
    ters to capitals, draw three lines under it, and
    write *caps.* in the margin.

2. Where there is a wrong letter, draw the pen
    through it, and make the right letter opposite
    in the margin.

3. A letter turned upside down.

4. The substitution of a comma for another point,
    or for a letter put in by mistake.

5. The insertion of a hyphen.

6. To draw close together the letters of a word that
    stand apart.

7. To take away a superfluous letter or word, the
    pen is struck through it and a round top *d* made
    opposite, being the contraction of *deleatur* ='ex-
    punge.'

8. Where a word has to be changed to Italic, draw a line under it, and write *Ital.* in the margin; and where a word has to be changed from Italic to Roman, write *Rom.* opposite.

9. When words are to be transposed, three ways of marking them are shown; but they are not usually numbered unless more than three words have their order changed.

10. The transposition of letters in a word.

11. To change one word for another.

12. The substitution of a period or a colon for any other point. It is customary to encircle these two points with a line.

13. The substitution of a capital for a small letter.

14. The insertion of a word or of a letter.

15. When a paragraph commences where it is not intended, connect the matter by a line, and write in the margin opposite *run on*.

16. Where a space or a quadrat stands up and appears, draw a line under it, and make a strong perpendicular line in the margin.

17. When a letter of a different size from that used, or of a different face, appears in a word, draw a line either through it or under it, and write opposite *w.f.*, for 'wrong fount.'

18. The marks for a paragraph, when its commencement has been omitted.

19. When a word or words have been struck out, and it is subsequently decided that they shall remain, make dots under them, and write the word *stet* in the margin.

20. The mark for a space where it has been omitted between two words.

21. To change a word from small letters to small capitals, make two lines under the word, and write *sm. caps.* opposite. To change a word from small capitals to small letters, make one line under the word, and write in the margin *lo. ca.*, for 'lower case.'

22. The mark for the apostrophe; and also the marks for inverted commas.

23. The manner of marking an omitted passage when it is too long to be written in the side margin. When this occurs, it may be written either at the top or the bottom of the page.

24. Marks when lines or words are not straight.

When corrected, the passage given above would read as follows—

ANTIQUITY, like every other quality that attracts the notice of mankind, has undoubtedly votaries that *reverence* it, not from reason, but from prejudice. Some seem to admire indiscriminately whatever has been long preserved, without considering that time has sometimes co-operated with chance: all perhaps are more willing to honour past than present excellence; and the mind contemplates genius through the shades of age, as the eye surveys the sun through artificial opacity. The great contention of criticism is to find the faults of the moderns and the beauties of the ancients. While an author is yet living, we estimate his powers by his worst performances; and when he is dead, we rate them by his best.

To works, however, of which the excellence is not absolute and definite, but gradual and comparative; to works, not raised upon principles demonstrative and scientific, but appealing wholly to observation and experience, no other test can be applied than LENGTH of duration and continuance of esteem.

Made in the USA
Monee, IL
07 July 2026